MW01492643

Art Basics for Children
The ABC's of Art

by

Sharon Jeffus

Visual Manna
P.O. Box 553
Salem, MO 65560
1-573-729-2100
http://www.visualmanna.com

Table of Contents

Using Supplies

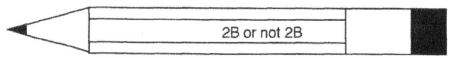

2B or not 2B

That is the question.

Drawing with pencils --- Soft pencils are the best to use for drawing. Always stress to children that they need to draw lightly in pencil first. If the student finds it too difficult to press lightly enough to make a light line with a soft pencil, they should try using a harder pencil such as a 4H for the primary sketch. I particularly recommend the Ebony drawing pencil for the final sketch. It is important to explore each of the styles for shading. Crosshatching, stroking, pointillism, and smudging need to be explored. It is always important to allow children to be as individualistic as possible in choosing their shading style. You will need a smudge stick (tortilla) for shading. In most cases you will need to exaggerate shading, as most people tend to not use enough contrast in their shading. I tell children to squint their eyes when they look at something to draw, this will help them see the contrast. I suggest beginning with a simple contour drawing, and then practice until a complete pencil painting (a picture done in great detail primarily with pencil) is completed. An alternate to the contour drawing would be to lightly define the space, shape and placement with circles.

> Did you know that there isn't any "LEAD" in a pencil? The "lead" is made up of graphite (carbon) and kaolinite (clay). The more clay, the harder the pencil. A 4H pencil has more clay than a 2H. B pencils are the softest, containing little clay.

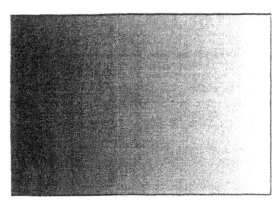

Charcoal is easily controlled by the amount of pressure applied.

Drawing with charcoal -- In my opinion, charcoal is primarily a shading medium.. Outline your subject lightly with pencil and then fill this in with charcoal paying close attention to contrast. Use white charcoal to accentuate light areas when you are working. As with pencil, the students will need to experiment with different strokes, techniques and smudging.

Using oil pastels -- Oil pastels are a wonderful medium for children. They love the bright colors. Encourage children to color darkly. You want the picture to look opaque, so you cannot see the white paper at all. Oil pastels are great to teach mixing of colors and are an introduction to oil painting. You can even take a cup of turpentine and brush and dip this into the colors to make the picture look like an oil painting.

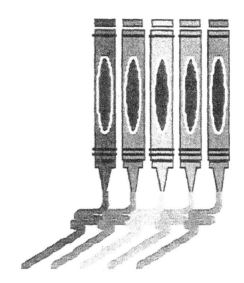

Using tempera paints --This is a delightful medium for children. Younger children or large groups of children experience great success using the plastic jar daubers. These are not messy because you paint with the sponge on the tip of the bottle. If you are using mixed tempera paints in an open container, add a little liquid detergent to the paint. This doesn't affect the color, but makes cleanup a lot easier. I believe baby food jars work best for storing paint. Baby food jars are also good to set on the table filled with clean water to clean brushes. The latest research shows that even young children can use various size paint brushes. Previously, younger children would only be given large brushes, now the research indicates children do better if they are given a variety of paintbrush sizes.

Using water color paint -- I believe it is best to use Prang water colors, or colors of a higher quality. Some of the cheaper water colors do not work well and fade over time. You need to stress with children when you teach watercolor, to work light. Use light colors because you can always get darker, but you cannot get lighter. Use your paper for the white color. The more water you use in proportion to the paint, the lighter your color will be. You can use salt, or a blow hair dryer for effect in your picture. You can take a toothbrush and splatter paint on your picture. There are many creative things you can do to enhance your pictures. Most of these come from trial and error, and must be experienced.

Using chalk pastels -- Many times chalk pastels are taught before learning oil or acrylic painting, because of the ability to mix this medium. Colored paper is often used to enhance the finished product. You need to tell students to use lots of chalk to achieve an opaque look. Blend and mix colors as much as possible. Layering colors works well. White and black charcoal pencils work well to detail your finished picture. I always like to start pastels with allowing students to make a sunset, showing many sunset pictures before they begin. This is good experience in mixing and blending. You can purchase pastel paper from a craft shop for your best work. Pastel paper or a very fine sand paper helps with achieving the opaque look. Using a smudge stick with pastels is an excellent suggestion for blending.

Modeling Compound-It is very important that children experience three-dimensional art experiences through clay, blocks, etc. Here are some recipes for modeling compound. Of course, you can go to a discount store and purchase modeling clay or play dough or you can make some yourself.

Sawdust clay
1 to 2 cups of sawdust
1 cup of wheat paste

mix with water and knead to get clay. Let clay air dry overnight or bake in oven at 350 degrees

Dough clay
4 tablespoons of flour
1 tablespoon of salt
2 tablespoons of water.

You can knead this dough and roll it out and make jewelry or magnet designs.

If you bake this dough mix at 350 degrees for 1 to 1 1/2 hours, you will have a hard dough sculpture you can paint.

Homemade play dough
1 cup flour
1/2 cup salt
2 teaspoons cream of tartar
      ---mix dry ingredients---
1 cup of water
1 teaspoon vegetable oil
food coloring.

Cook complete mixture for two or three minutes and then knead.

Silly Putty
2 parts white craft glue to 1 part liquid starch.

When you mix this together, let it dry.

Edible clay
1 cup smooth peanut butter
1 1/3 cups of powered milk
3 tablespoons honey.

Mix in a bowl. You are ready to sculpt and eat!

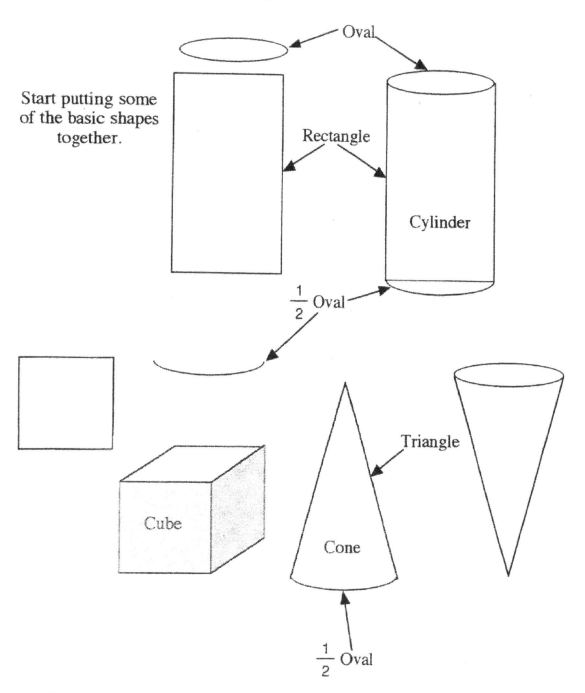

Start putting some of the basic shapes together.

Oval

Oval

Rectangle

Cylinder

$\frac{1}{2}$ Oval

Cube

Triangle

Cone

$\frac{1}{2}$ Oval

A good way to enhance your fine motor skills is to practice making circles and sharp "M's" keeping them between the lines, (see below).

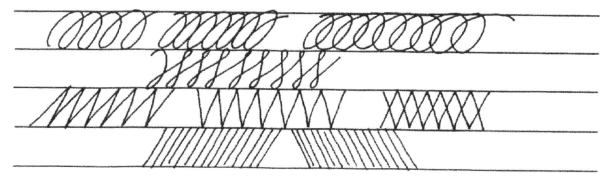

Learning Basic Shapes

Make this elephant using the basic shapes below. Every time the child makes a shape, say the name of the shape. This will reinforce learning basic geometric shapes.

SQUARE   RECTANGLE   TRIANGLE

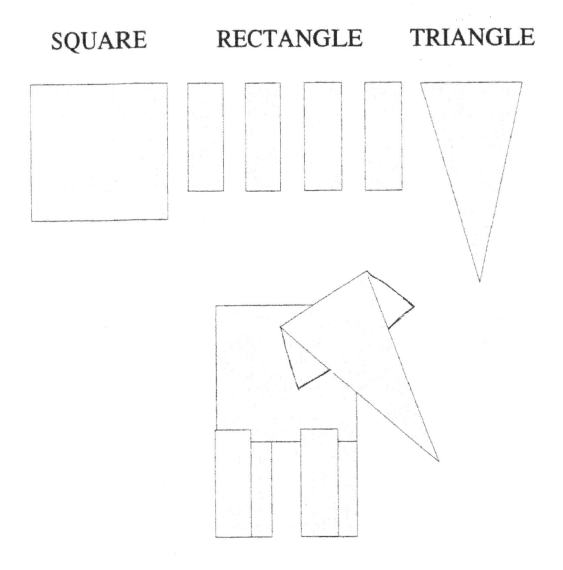

INTRODUCTION

THIS BOOK OF **A**RT **B**ASICS FOR **C**HILDREN IS AN ENJOYABLE WAY TO LEARN ART BASICS FOR BEGINNERS IN ART AND YOUNGER CHILDREN. EACH CHILD IS LIKE A SNOWFLAKE, WITH AN INDIVIDUAL STYLE TO BE ENCOURAGED. ON THE FOLLOWING PAGES YOU WILL SEE A BRIEF INTRODUCTION AND PROGRESSION OF FOUR STYLES OF ART. SHOWING CHILDREN GREAT WORKS OF ART WILL HELP THEM TO BE ENCOURAGED AND UNDERSTAND THAT EVERY ARTIST IS UNIQUE AND HAS THEIR OWN STYLE. USING ART SUPPLIES AND A STUDY OF BASIC SHAPES BEGIN THIS BOOK. THEN, WITHIN THE FRAMEWORK OF THE **ABC**'S, ART TECHNIQUES AND VOCABULARY ARE TAUGHT. A GOOD ART TEACHER IS LIKE A CHEERLEADER, ENCOURAGING CHILDREN TO NEW HEIGHTS OF CREATIVITY. IT IS SUGGESTED YOU DO THE BOOK IN CHRONOLOGICAL ORDER, READING OVER THE BASIC SHAPES AND USING SUPPLIES FIRST. ENJOY ART!

MAKING A BIRD USING BASIC SHAPES

Make a bird using the following shapes.

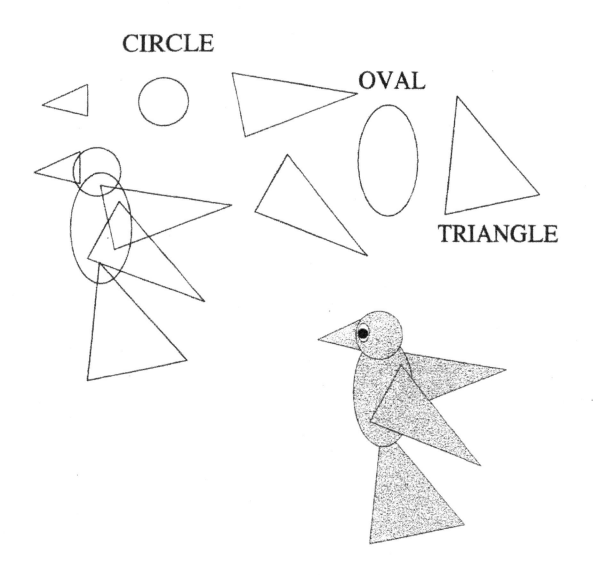

CIRCLE

OVAL

TRIANGLE

MAKING A CATERPILLAR

Use the following shapes to make a caterpillar.

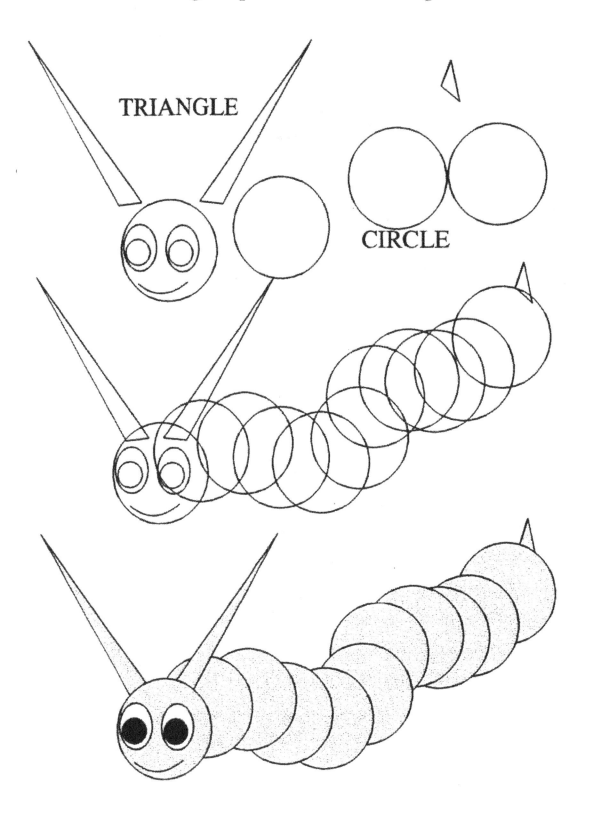

TRIANGLE

CIRCLE

MAKING A FROG

Use these basic geometric shapes to make a frog.

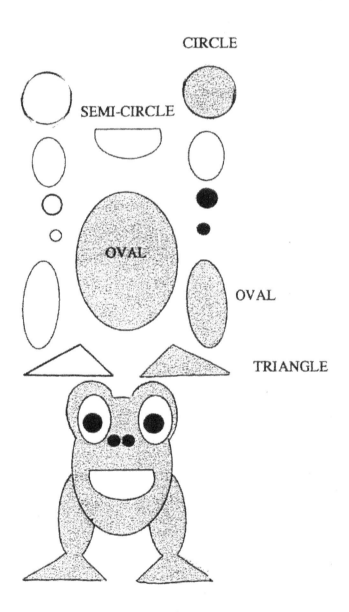

CIRCLE

SEMI-CIRCLE

OVAL

OVAL

TRIANGLE

MAKING A WHALE

Use these geometric shapes to make a whale.

RECTANGLE   OVAL   TRIANGLE

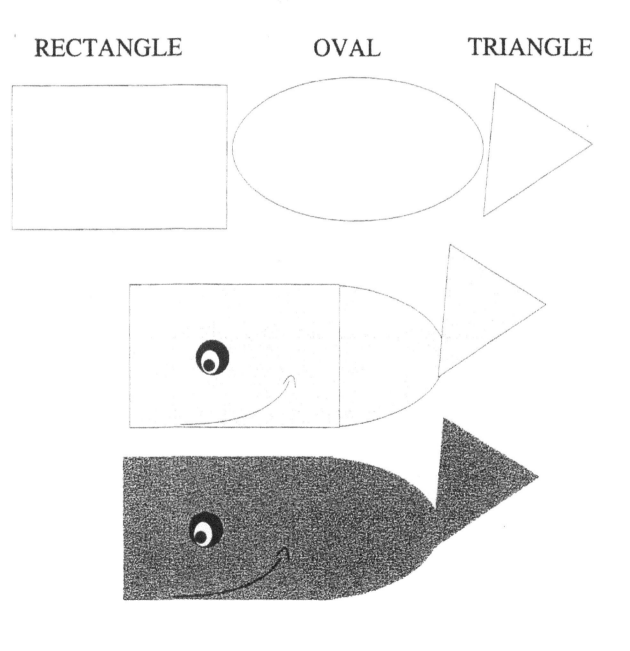

The Color Wheel

The three primary colors are red, yellow and blue. The three secondary colors are orange, green and violet. Colors opposite each other on the color wheel are complementary colors.

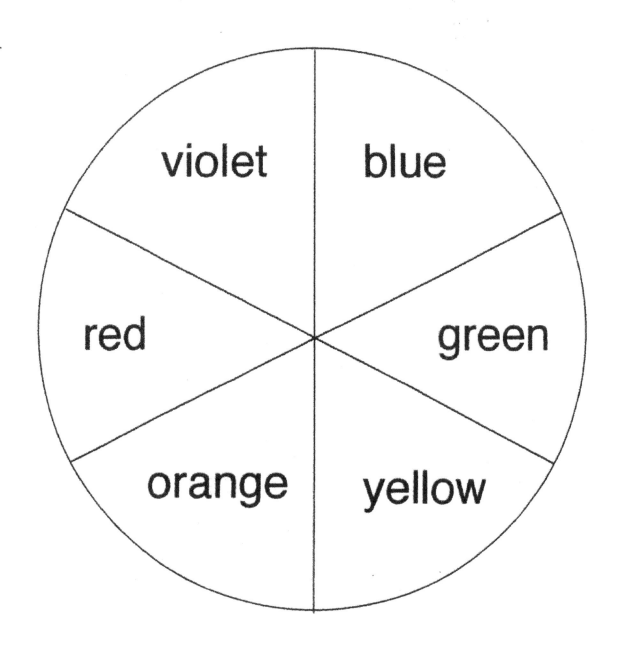

Lesson 1

Drawing requires observation and practice.

color wheel

Make a circle.

A is for apple.

Observe an apple carefully.

Apples are usually red. Red is a primary color on the color wheel. Red is a hot color. What do you get when you mix red and white? You get pink. Pink is a pastel color. Can you think of any other pastel colors?

How do you make your apple look round? You shade your apple. Follow these simple directions to shade an apple.

Draw an apple on a table.

Lesson 2

B is for ball.

Can you draw a ball?

PATTERNS

Draw a circle first. Can you draw a ball with a pattern on it? A soccer ball has a pattern on it. Shade your ball with a pattern the same way you shaded your apple. Design a ball and invent a special game. Put a pattern on your ball.

Yellow is a primary color. Yellow is a hot color. Make your ball's pattern in red and yellow. These two colors are both primary colors. There are only three primary colors. All the colors are made from these colors. Can you guess what the other primary color is? Turn the page.

GEOMETRIC BALL

Lesson 3

C
is for cat

The foreground is made up of objects in the front of a picture. The background are things in the distance. You can make a cat by using a circle and triangle. Follow the simple directions to make a cat.

 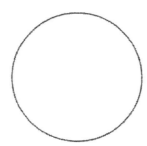 

Can you make a picture of a cat? Put your cat in the foreground by making it larger. Put a tree in the background. We have been talking about the color wheel. One of the three primary colors is blue. Make the sky in your picture blue.

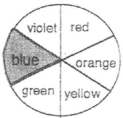

Lesson 4

D is for dog

Texture is how something feels. When you make something look like it has texture, you have created an implied texture. Artists make the fur on animals look like real fur.

You can make a dog by drawing ovals. Follow these simple steps to make a dog using ovals. When you are finished, make lines to show the fur on the dog. When this fur really looks like fur, you have created an implied texture.

Lesson 5

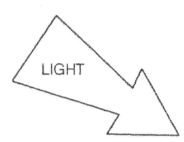

E is for egg.

An egg is in an oval shape. Draw an oval
shape. Using patterns from Lesson 2, draw a
repeated design on the shell of your egg. This
will turn your egg into a wonderful Easter egg.
Next shade it from just one light source. This
will give it a solid three dimensional look. See
the sample picture.

E is also for elephant.

Look at the sample of how to draw an elephant on
the next page. Shade the elephant the same way
you shaded the egg.

Just for fun, draw a picture of an elephant trying to
hatch an egg. An elephant is a mammal, so it
bears its young live. Can you name any other
characteristics of a mammal?

HOW TO DRAW AN
ELEPHANT

Lesson 6

F
is for feather

A feather is just one of the patterns in nature. A feather is made up of lines that are repeated. Can you draw a feather that will look so real that it looks like you could pick if up off of the paper? A flamingo is a bird that begins with an F. This bird is made of feathers. Look at the flamingo. Can you draw this bird looking at the directions? Can you make the feathers really look like feathers? Flamingos are pink. When you mix red and white you get pink. Pink is a pastel color. When you add white to a color on the color wheel, you get a pastel color.

Use circles to define the space.

Draw the shape lightly.

Darken the lines you want to keep. Erase the construction lines (circles.) Add details.

Lesson 7

G is for grapes

Can you make a bunch of circles together overlapping? When you look at a group of grapes, you see overlapping circles together. If possible, go to the grocery store and purchase a bunch of grapes. Draw your grapes carefully on a flat surface. When you are finished, shade your circles to look round.

overlap

Grapes are violet (purple). Violet is made by mixing red and blue together. On a color wheel, colors opposite each other are complementary colors. Grapes are violet and circles. The sun is a circle shape and is yellow. Yellow and violet are complementary colors. Make a picture of a bright yellow sun shining down on some purple grapes. You will have a picture using complementary colors.

Lesson 8

The horizon line is the place where the sky and land meet.

H is for horizon line.

You always want to put an horizon line on the paper when you draw an outdoor scene. One point perspective is seen when you put an horizon line in the distance and have a road going towards the horizon line. Two parallel lines always meet at a point on the horizon line. See example. Make a picture of a highway that meets at a point in the distance. Have the picture show a beautiful sunset. Use hot colors in your sky for the sunset. Hot colors are red, yellow and orange.

violet
blue
green
orange
yellow

HORIZON LINE ➚

H is also for hands.

This picture of hands is done by Leonardo da Vinci, one of the most famous artists of all time. He was an artist of the Renaissance time period. Trace around your hand with a pencil. Now put as much detail on the hand as you can.

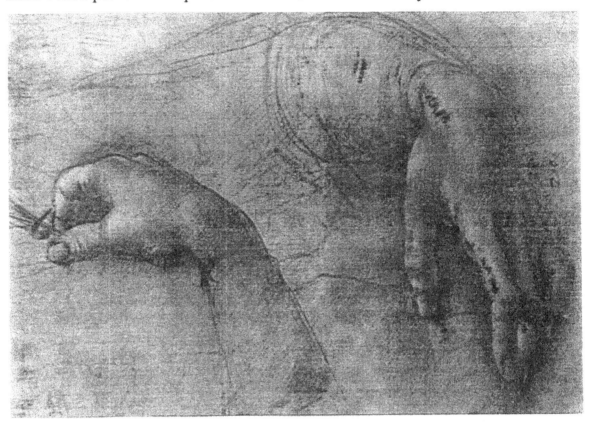

Lesson 9

I is for island.

An island is a freeform shape. Look at the picture of the island with palm trees on both sides. This picture has formal balance. A palm tree is very easy to draw. Practice drawing the palm tree. Now draw a horizon line. This will be where the water and sky meet. Put an island in the water. Now put a palm tree on one side of the island. Put an identical palm tree on the other side. You will have a picture with formal balance.

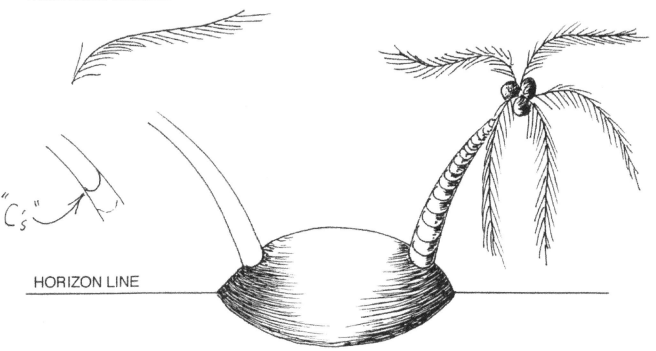

"C's"

HORIZON LINE

Lesson 10

J
J is for jar

It is easy to draw a glass jar. Find a glass jar to observe. You will notice that it is transparent. A bubble is transparent. A window is transparent. When you shade a jar or glass, you can shade with your pencil and then use your eraser to make the jar look like glass. When you draw windows, you can use diagonal lines to make them look like glass. See the examples.

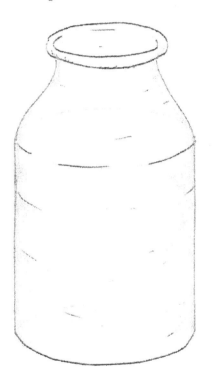

Lesson 11

K is for kaleidoscope

Design is the arrangement of form, color and shapes to produce a complete and artistic composition.

A kaleidoscope is a tube shaped instrument containing little bits of colored glass and plastic reflected by mirrors. You see a symmetrical design made up of various patterns created by moving the tube. The colors and patterns are constantly changing. Can you remember looking into a kaleidoscope? Use a compass and make a circle that fills your paper. Now use the compass to make an interesting abstract design. Do the design in pencil first and then color it in in bright colors. When you are finished, laminate the circle with a laminator or clear contact paper.

Note: Developing fine motor skills is an important aspect of a good elementary art program. Some children love to color. This can be a fun way to enhance fine motor development. It is preferable to allow children to create their own designs. Coloring book designs already created by a professional artist (called dictated art) tend to limit creativity. Dictated art can cause children to say, "I can't draw." When what they mean is, I can't draw like a professional artist. Children's art is often fresh and simple. Even the professional artist had to start somewhere, and all we (or our children) need is the encouraging words.

Lesson 12

L is for line.

HORIZONTAL

V
E
R
T
I
C
A
L

D
I
A
G
O
N
A
L

There are three different lines that we can mention. A horizontal line is a line that goes from side to side. A vertical line goes up and down. A diagonal line is slanted. When you want to show movement, you use a diagonal line. Look at the sample picture done entirely in line. Look up Vincent Van Gogh in the encyclopedia. His brushstrokes were so heavy that it looked like his pictures were done in lines. Do a line design similar to the sample picture shown.

Lesson 13

M is for monochrome.

Monochrome means a picture, especially a painting, done in different shades of a single color.

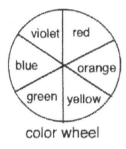

color wheel

A monochromatic color scheme is one in which the artist takes one color from the color wheel and mixes black and white with this to color his complete picture. "M" can also be for mountain. When you do a picture of a mountain, you are doing a landscape. Draw a picture similar to the one below on a piece of white paper 12" by 18." Now paint or color the picture in chalk or oil pastels using just one color and black and white.

Lesson 14

N is for negative space.

If you make an object in white and surround the object in black, the black is negative space. If you do a picture of a full moon in a black sky, you can easily recognize the positive and negative space. Look at the sample below. Now do a picture in black and white, of a snowman at night, silhouetted by a full moon.

15

Lesson 15

O is for opaque.

Op art is when you use color or line and create an optical illusion.

Something that you cannot see through is opaque. When you are using certain supplies in art, you need to color so that your color is opaque. You will need to color very hard. You do not want any white to show through. This is true when you work with oil pastels and chalk pastels. Many times you need to be careful as you color with markers to make sure no white shows through. Op art is when you use color or line and create an optical illusion. This can be done in various ways. When you put two pure complementary colors together in repeated areas, sometimes there is the appearance of movement. You can also use lines to create movement. Look at the following optical design. Now make your own.

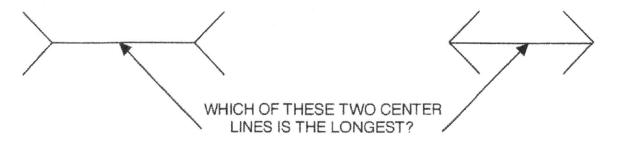

WHICH OF THESE TWO CENTER LINES IS THE LONGEST?

Lesson 16

P
is for pointillism.

> **Pointillism is the method of coloring a canvas with tiny dots of pure color.**

 Pointillism is a wonderful style of art that uses small splotches of color or dots to create a picture. George Suerat was the first artist to use pointillism. Look at the sample picture. Now make a picture only using dots. Do the picture first using only black dots. Now do the same picture using colored dots. A way to do this quickly is to use crayons and color a picture on a piece of coarse sandpaper. Now turn the paper over on a piece of white construction paper and iron with a medium heat iron. Instant pointillism!

"P" is also for pyramid.

Lesson 17

Q is for quilt.

A quilt is defined as a bedspread that is filled with layers of cloth filled with
cotton, wool, etc. It is stitched together in lines and patterns. Many times quilts
are treated as special Ozark Mountain Art. Large prices are paid for intricately
designed quilts. Talented seamstresses take beautiful fabrics and put them together
in an interesting design. It is a wonderful thing to see a contour drawing of a bird
or log cabin on a quilt, and then have the shape filled in with patterns and colors.
A contour line is a line that goes around a shape. Have children do a contour
drawing by allowing them to look at a particular grouping of objects. Now have
them draw the objects without looking at their paper or pencil. This will help them
when they draw it the second time, to really look at and observe the lines.

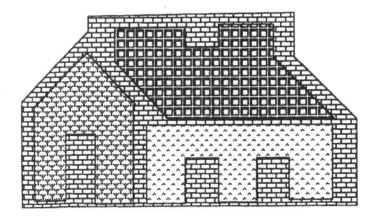

Q is also for queen.

A portrait is a realistic picture of a person. Look at the portrait of Queen Elizabeth. Can you draw a portrait of Elizabeth? Follow the simple directions for the proportions of the face and practice drawing a face. Can you do a picture of yourself as a king/queen?

DRAWING THE FACE
IN PROPORTION

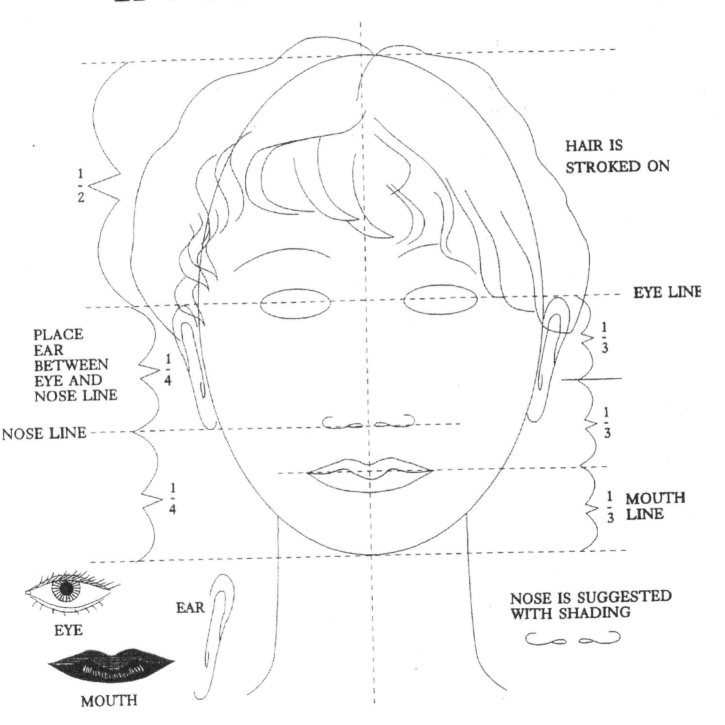

HAIR IS
STROKED ON

EYE LINE

$\frac{1}{2}$

PLACE
EAR
BETWEEN
EYE AND
NOSE LINE

$\frac{1}{4}$

$\frac{1}{3}$

NOSE LINE

$\frac{1}{3}$

$\frac{1}{4}$

$\frac{1}{3}$ MOUTH
LINE

EYE

EAR

NOSE IS SUGGESTED
WITH SHADING

MOUTH

Lesson 18

R is for Rembrandt.

Rembrandt is well known for his use of positive and negative space and extreme contrasts. Chiaroscuro (ke äro skoo´ro), is the dramatic use of lights and dark to create depth as seen in this picture *The Man With the Golden Helmet* .

You can go to your local garden center and ask for some flowers that bloom at night. Ask for the evening primrose, moon flowers, cereus, or datura, just to name a few. Around July, the plants from these night blooming flowers will bloom. Nocturnal moths pollinate these plants, just like bees and butterflies pollinate daytime flowers. Many of these flowers are light or white colored and contrast against the black background. Talk about positive and negative space. The night sky is the negative space and the white flowers are

the positive space. Have younger children use black background paper and make a torn picture design by tearing flowers and leaves out of white and green paper. They can even use light colored oil pastels and color a night moth on the picture. Show older students several pictures by Rembrandt. His use of positive and negative space is dramatic. Have older students use tempera paint and paint a nighttime picture with the white flowers and the moth shining in the darkness.

Lesson 19

To produce gradation of light or color in a drawing or picture is shading.

S is for shading.

Practice different kinds of shading with your pencil. You can use a smudge stick (tortilla) to smudge your picture. You can shade by stroking or crosshatching. A pencil painting is a picture done entirely in pencil. The sky is colored in pencil, and everything in the picture is varying pencil shades---black to light gray to white. S is also for seascape. You can do a pencil painting of a seascape. Look at the seascape below and try to use your pencil to duplicate it.

Lesson 20

T is for texture.

Texture is how something feels. T is also for turtle. Look at the picture of the turtle. Notice the pattern on his back. The turtle has a leather-like texture. Do you suppose you can create this with a pencil. Applying pressure to the pencil allows you to get different shades and values.   If you can get the turtle shell to look like it has texture, you have created an implied texture. When you have attempted to draw the picture in pencil, now color your turtle with oil pastels or chalks.

Lesson 21

U

is for underwater.

U is also for under painting. When you learn to do acrylic or oil painting, depending on the method you learn, you will learn about under painting. When I started painting, my teacher wanted me to paint my entire painting beige with a touch of pink before I started my painting. This is called under painting. It can tie your picture together. Sometimes it is preferable to using a white canvas. You can also begin your picture in chalk pastels by coloring your white paper a color before you begin. When you design your composition, and color it, sometimes you will see some of the under painting coming through. Did you notice that many times chalk or charcoal paper is a pastel color.? Start an underwater picture in water color by adding a slight tinge of green to your jar of water and painting your entire picture a light shade of green. Let this dry. Now draw your underwater scene. Paint the scene completely, including painting the water blue.

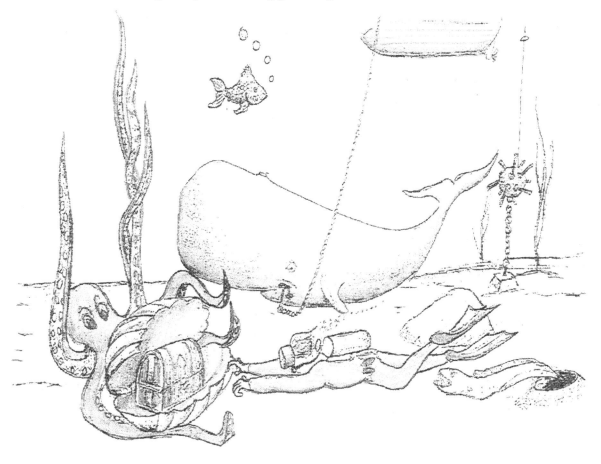

Lesson 22

V

is for violets.

The word violet can have two meanings. Of course, there is the cool color of violet that you get when you mix red and blue. It is opposite yellow on the color wheel. Next, we can think of the lovely flowers that are called violets. We can draw flowers by remembering that good drawing requires observation and practice. A good exercise in drawing is to get a vase of flowers, preferably violets, and then cut out a window and zero in on one section of the flowers at a time. When you draw by carefully looking and seeing the details of the flowers, it will help your picture look realistic. Violet and yellow are complementary colors. Make a picture of violet flowers with a yellow background.

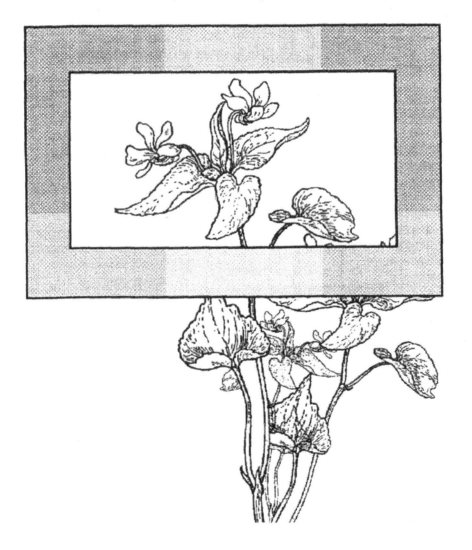

Lesson 23

W is also for watercolor.

> A technique is the way in which the fundamentals of an artistic work are handled.

Watercolor paint is a pigment that is mixed with water. It is a tricky medium to use. There are a few hints that will work well when using watercolor. When you do water color, always work very light. You can always use washes of light colors to get darker, but is very difficult to get lighter. I believe that David Plank, one of the best water color artists I know uses white paper and light with amazing sensitivity. He works very light, and his pictures have a transparent beauty. There are several different techniques to watercolor. You will want something to blot your paper. You will need to purchase special water color paper. Use a sponge to sponge different areas. You can also sprinkle salt on a part of your picture for an interesting effect. You can also use a straw and blow the water for a windy effect. You will need a wide brush and a detail brush. Make a whale in watercolor. Paint a blue under painting for your whale first and let this dry, now finish your picture by putting on the whale and the ocean waves. If you can obtain some white tempera paint and sponge your picture for foam on the waves, that would be wonderful. Look at the picture of the whale below. A whale is an easy subject for a watercolor. Do a picture of a whale in pencil first. Try to get a wavy effect with the water.

Lesson 24

 is for X-ray.

When you X-ray the human body, you see the skeletal system. When drawing the human body, you need to study the bones and muscles. Look at this skeletal drawing by Leonardo da Vinci. He was a great artist who studied the bones and muscles of human cadavers to learn the proportions of the human body. A child's head is larger in proportion to his body. Study and observe the proportions of the bodies of adults and children in several magazines before you begin. Generally, lightly sketching a body in circles and ovals gives the artist a feel for the proportions. Use the eraser and adjust as needed and then draw in the details.

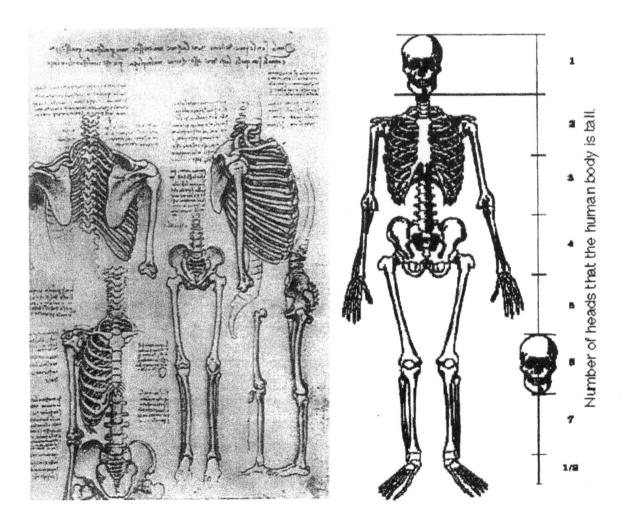

Number of heads that the human body is tall.

1 2 3 4 5 6 7 1/2

Lesson 25

Y is for yellow.

Lines coming out
from the center
are radial lines.

The sun is yellow. Sun symbols have been very famous throughout history. Most young children make a sun symbol by taking a circle and drawing lines coming out from it. These lines are called radial lines. A symbol is something that stands for or represents something else. Can you think of any symbol in advertising? Look at the sun symbol below. Make your own sun symbol and color it with hot colors---red, yellow and orange. You can even give your sun texture by adding salt to yellow tempera paint and painting your sun. Adding human characteristics to inanimate objects is called personification. Can you give your sun a big smile?

Lesson 26

Z is for zebra.

There are several interesting facts in art about the zebra. Did you know that black, white, brown and gray are neutral colors. A zebra is colored with neutral colors.

Sometimes I wonder if all the pictures of the dinosaurs that we see might be wrong in their use of color after I see the zebra. If you ever dug up the bones of a zebra, could you imagine the animal would be black and white striped? A stripe is a pattern. One of my favorite color combinations are black and white and blue and green. Follow the simple instructions and draw a zebra in the

foreground of your picture. Make the grass green and the sky blue. Now make a zebra the same way, but make this using only black and hot colors. He will be silhouetted on the horizon line in a sunset picture. The sunset will be in yellow, orange and red. If you study Africa, you will see that it has spectacular sunsets.

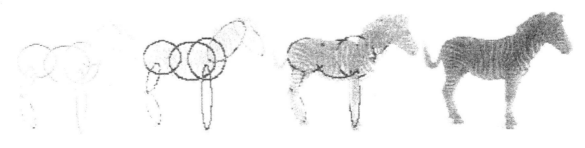

Realistic

This realistic picture of a woman by Leonardo da Vinci is an excellent example of the realistic style. Before the development of the camera, artists pictured things as they appear to be. Realistic art looks like a photo and has lots of details. Artists recorded great moments and history and showed us what kings and important people in history looked like. Realism is still popular today. Most wildlife art is realistic. Have children do their best to make a picture that looks exactly like something really is.

Impressionism

This wonderful picture of a woman at the piano is a representation of a picture by the great Impressionistic artist Renoir. Impressionism is recognized by a lack of detail. If you would just glance at a scene and look away, you have an idea of what an Impressionistic picture is like. A good project to understand Impressionism is to draw a scene lightly in pencil first. Now use sponges or daubers and complete the picture in colors.

Expressionism

This picture by Matisse is an excellent example of Expressionism. An Expressionistic picture is an expression of the inner feelings of the artist. The colors can be totally distorted. Trees can be orange, lakes can be pink. Paint a picture of your favorite place. Draw what it looks like, and then color it how you feel about it.

Abstract Art

Abstract art is nonobjective. It is a composition of lines and designs that come together in a composition, looking like nothing from real life. See if you can think of a title for a work of art. Let's say you choose to do an abstract picture called "Parade." Now do a picture showing how you feel about a parade in shapes and patterns.

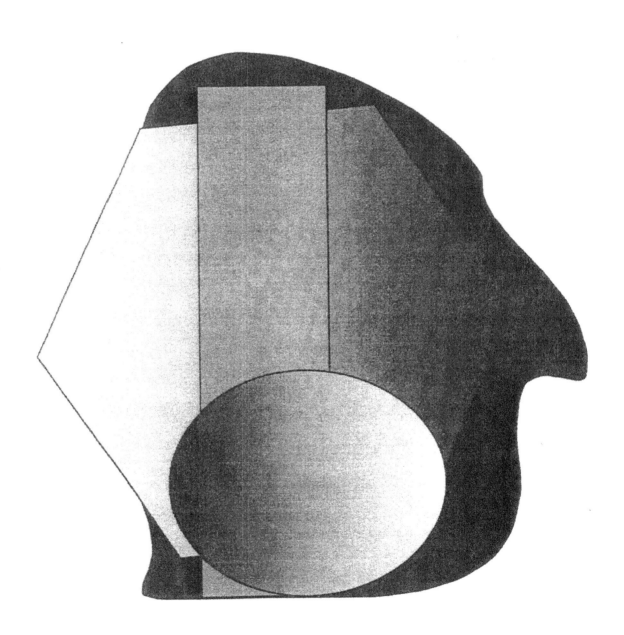

MORE BOOKS FROM VISUAL MANNA

Art Through the Core series...

Teaching American History Through Art
Teaching Astronomy Through Art
Teaching English Through Art
Teaching History Through Art
Teaching Literature Through Art
Teaching Math Through Art
Teaching Science Through Art
Teaching Social Studies Through Art

Other Books...

Art Adventures in Narnia
Art Basics for Children
Bible Arts & Crafts
Christian Holiday Arts & Crafts
Dragons, Dinosaurs, Castles and Knights
Drawing, Painting and Sculpting Horses
Expanding Your Horizons Through Words
Indians In Art
Master Drawing
Preschool & Early Elementary Art Basics
Preschool Bible Lessons
Visual Manna 1: Complete Art Curriculum
Visual Manna 2: Advanced Techniques

Books available at Rainbow Resource Center:
www.rainbowresource.com • 888.841.3456

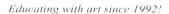

Educating with art since 1992!

A Christian is one whose imagination should fly beyond the stars. Francis Schaeffer

HIS LIONS

Contact *visualmanna@gmail.com* if you are interested in our Intern program. Students learn how to teach art, do murals for ministry, prepare an excellent portfolio, and much more. Go to **visualmanna.com** for information.

Free art lessons are available at **OurHomeschoolForum.com** and books are available at Rainbow Resource Center (**www.rainbowresource.com**). Try all our "Art Through the Core" series and other books as well! Make learning fun for kids!!! Sharon Jeffus teaches Art Intensives in person for the Landry Academy at **landryacademy.com**.

Made in the USA
Coppell, TX
22 August 2022

81831876R00031